MATTER / MOTHER

ALSO BY THE AUTHOR

Memory Keeper

Origin Stories

Singing to the Bones

Matter / Mother

poems by

APRIL TIERNEY

WAYFARER
BASED IN THE PIONEER VALLEY, MASS.

WAYFARER BOOKS

WWW.WAYFARERBOOKS.ORG

Published in 2024 by Wayfarer Books & Homebound Publications
Cover Design and Interior Design by Connor L. Wolfe
TRADE PAPERBACK 978-1-956368-99-4
EBOOK 978-1-956368-96-3

10 9 8 7 6 5 4 3 2 1

Look for our titles in paperback, ebook, and audiobook wherever books are sold.
Wholesale offerings for retailers available through Ingram.

Wayfarer Books is committed to ecological stewardship.
We greatly value the natural environment and invest in conservation.

PO Box 1601, Northampton, MA 01060

wayfarer@homeboundpublications.com

HOMEBOUNDPUBLICATIONS.COM & WAYFARERBOOKS.ORG

For my Mother,
Sue Rusch

Matter n. from Latin *māteria* substance from which something is made, from *māter* origin, source, Mother.

TABLE OF CONTENTS

INTRODUCTION

I wrote these poems during the first two and a half years of my daughter's life. Most days while she napped, I labored to bring forth some of the stories and realities of Mothering within an anthropocentric, capitalistic, nuclear family paradigm—stories that have often been repressed or dismissed. This is the book that I longed to read in that early postpartum time, but which I could not find. It is raw, dark, truthful, and redemptive.

My love of the Earth has informed much of this writing, as well as the way that I have wrestled with many of the questions presented here. There is a memory that lives in my bones, where, in Earth-based cultures, Mothers are held at the center. As life-bearers, they are treated with the same care and respect as Mother Earth. However, in industrialized societies where the Earth is both exploited and neglected, Mothers are, too. As if this were not sorrowing enough, we Mothers often internalize our struggles as personal inadequacies, rather than something that is culturally imposed. Throughout this body of work, I am endeavoring to shed light on the times we are living and Mothering within, to hopefully redirect some accountability as well as to bring reverence back to the life-bearers and the stories we carry.

I would never attempt to speak for all Mothers' experiences. Not only would this be disrespectful, but it would involve a kind of arrogance I do not have. There are a million ways to Mother; within these poems and prose poems, I stumble my way through a few of them. I am writing from my embodied experience as a new Mother within the dominant culture of North America, whose ancestors immigrated here from Germany, Russia, Latvia, and Poland. My experience may not be translatable to other cultures, circumstances, or ways of being. There may be similarities, and bless the similarities, but I stand equally for the differences. I stand for there being a multitude of ways to inhabit this role. I do not believe there is one right way.

As you read, you will notice that Mother is always capitalized, which is to challenge the Christocentric paradigm wherein only father receives this distinction. You will also notice that I occasionally employ the slash symbol (as in the title) to acknowledge how an idea, person, or place can actually be two things at once.

Finally, as a writer, I am taught to be specific, to steer away from generalizations and abstractions. And as a woman, I long to stand inside of my own story, since we have so often been written out of the history books. I come from a lineage of storytellers. My paternal Grandmother was the most skilled storyteller I have ever met. She knew when to embellish and what to leave out. She was not afraid of using strong language or expressing her opinion. Listening to her long-winded narratives was my education, my inheritance. So now, in your hands, you hold some of my most revealing stories. They are also stories of the Earth and our more-than-human kin. May they be lanterns for your darkest nights. May they whisper back to you of your own strength, the beauty and necessity of your own narratives, which I long to hear, too.

April Tierney

Lyons, Colorado / May 2024

BIRTH STORY

If you had not been an animal before, in labor you became
animal—hoofed and horned, howling into the fist of day or night

or many days and many nights. You became all hands and knees,
hips and deafening heart. You became strong and sometimes scared,
but mostly a raucous wonderment of determination, of power,
of everything that is holy in this world. You became breath

spiraling in and out, you traveled way beyond those agonizing hours
into Deep Time, to the place your Grandmothers birthed and continue
to birth, where they blessed your bones and helped your body to open.

You became the prayers and songs of every mountain and river,
each valley and gust of wind, all the stars shooting across
the night sky since the beginning of time. You became.

And now you have landed back in a body that is unfamiliar to you,
uncomfortable within the constraints of civilization. People ooh and aah
at your baby, but you still have horns. They do not acknowledge the horns.
You will never again be that same woman who walked in a straight line,

you have been initiated into the land of fire and rough magic,
fur and darkness. You looked into death's lustful eyes and
held your life in full view, even as your life turned to ash,
you kept holding, even as you did not know how to go on,

you went on. Very few people will ask about your story,
yet you will become your story. You will live into a body
that is informed by the rhythms of water and lightning,
you will no longer walk from here to there, you will prowl—

your tail will swing back and forth, your ears
will be forever tuned to what is happening
over the hill, to the thundering in the distance.

MOTHER CANADA GOOSE

During spring, Canada geese fly northward
in their great V's above the Colorado Rockies.
The bowed shape of prayer is all but useless
to us at this time of year—we throw our heads
and hearts back instead, looking up to behold them—
a skein of benediction soaring across our western sky.

Invariably, one loyal pair always stops to nest
at the algae covered pond in my rural neighborhood.
A few years ago I saw the Mother goose scouting
out that sanctified place where she would eventually
create refuge for her young. She stood atop a big boulder
on the hill above our house, calling out, claiming
her part in the profound story unfurling before us.

The day I saw her I was eight months pregnant,
waddling along with equal parts awe and apprehension.
She stood strong and proud on the very same boulder
that I sat in front of one year prior while fasting and praying
for a vision—three long days and nights out on the land
audaciously asking the world if I was meant to become
a Mother. I wrestled with this question for a long time

fearing for the mess that future generations would inherit,
wondering if it was wise or kind to bring more life
onto this broken and overpopulated planet.
When I finally decided to go up onto the mountain,
I promised my husband that I would say yes
to whatever answer came faithfully through the trees,
the bees, the wind, the rocks, and the rain.

So on that third day when I saw the face of our future child
emerge from the same boulder that this Mother goose
now stands upon after flying hundreds of miles
to find her nest, I knew my bones were fiercely blessed.

But I also wondered, did the goose ever question if this
changing world would be viable enough to support her young?
Did fear or doubt ever enter her hollow-boned body,
haunt her dreams, alter her patterns of flight?

I do not know the answers to these questions,
but I do know that she chose the pond carefully,
that she found someplace quiet and kind
for her five downy goslings to grow into
robust and brave birds so that they could
make their mighty journey south come winter.

I know that our children grew
into the world alongside one other.
I know that she and I are life-bearers
and that without us, there is no story
to tell. I know that when her family
eventually flew from the pond,
I missed them terribly

and that my daughter will hear tales
about their elegance and intelligence
for as long as there is wind in my lungs.

WOMAN ON A THRESHOLD

You have given your life over to something
that is bigger than you, that will ask
unspeakable things of you

yet you will learn how to speak them,
you will not allow silence to be the story
that swells around your howling heart.

You are not entirely sure what you have said yes to.
It is mysterious, the extent and depth of it,
the beauty and darkness. Even still, you say yes.

You are not afraid of mysterious things,
you have been honed by them, strengthened
by them, humbled and made human—

you yourself are a mysterious thing.

Even to call it a threshold seems too small,
it is a horizon and you are dancing toward it.

You cannot see the sun from here
but you keep dancing—

you trust your body because your body is strong,
you trust your intuition because you are a woman
and you have been dancing all of your life.

You have gone within
and you have gone without,

you sat beneath the stars
praying and listening,

you slept there
and when you woke

wind was in your hair,
a wild myth in your eyes.

You cannot lose yourself
because you know yourself.

You know endings and beginnings,
you know how to belong to this world,
how to make sacred all of your days.

THIS BODY, AN ALTAR

Sorrow is the sound that reverberates through every cell
and each quiet hour, though so is the precision of joy.

A Mother's body is the birthplace of paradox,
both desire and satisfaction have a home here—
there is no end to the feelings, only beginnings.

But how do you create an identity from that? How do you
dress yourself in the morning and proclaim to the world,
"This is the woman that I bled and stretched and danced
with death to become?" Maybe identities are overrated,
maybe they are all too often co-opted into Gods.

I think I will relish being free of an identity for awhile,
even though I go by so many different names.
I think I will walk through my days naked,
this body a flame, a holy altar to make offerings to,
a sacred site from which new life springs.

THE MILK GODDESS

"Who is She?" I ask.
"The Milk Goddess," they say.
"Do not look directly at Her
or you will turn into fire."

But I can not resist and so
my eyes start to burn.

I wake a thousand times
a night, trying to climb
my way back to you,

trying to learn how
to inhabit the image

that has set flame
to everything

inside of me.

MAMA

"Mama," was my daughter's first word,
she tossed it across the room like an arrow,
its honed edge splintered my heart

and Rumi wrote, "The wound is where the light
enters you." I have so much more light in me now.

Somedays I do not recognize myself in this new name,
"Mama," though she stares directly at me while saying it,
though she reaches out to me if I am across the room
like I was never meant to be so far away, though she
wraps her tiny body around mine when I am close

like she is still a part of my body, like we did not
become two beings at birth. Every day I lay her down
onto the Earth so that she knows I am not her only Mother,
so that she can feel the ground breathing beneath her, holding
her, drinking in her tears and transforming them into flowers.

Now, when she says, "Mama," she isn't only looking at me,
she is tossing arrows out into the heart of the world,
though I still run to her when she falls and cries, "Mama,"

as big, fat tears roll down her cheeks,
as she points to the place that hurts
and asks me to kiss it, to take away the pain,
to sprout up inside of that name and become

the sheltering tree, the nutrient rich soil,
the nectar inside of the flowers, inside
of the bee's mouths, inside of the world.

THE PROGENY OF LOVE

A magnificent killer whale named Tahlequah
gave birth and caught the world's attention.
Her calf died only thirty minutes after being born,
each of those blessed minutes a sacrament
to the progeny of love. But the real reason

journalists and photographers and millions of viewers
followed this Mother's story, was her willingness to grieve
unbidden, to become a thing utterly governed by kinship.

After a year and a half of growing this enormous life
inside of her belly, and the immense feat of labor,
and half an hour of looking into one another's eyes,
Tahlequah proceeded to carry her dead baby
on the tip of her nose for seventeen days,
traveling more than a thousand miles
all throughout the Salish Sea.

And some people think that grief is not
inexplicably beautiful. But perhaps it's because
those people (who are us people) no longer see
grieving enacted publicly as a plea for sanity,
as a way of feeding that which grants us life.

There was no real grieving at my Mother's funeral—
sniffling and shoving tears back up into our eyes, yes,
but no keening. No collapsing into the bottomless cavern
of one another's trembling arms, no crying out
into the insufferable heat of that late-summer day,
and certainly no carrying my Mom's dead body
as a holy procession all throughout the places
she ever knew and loved. So I continued to carry her

mostly on my own. I wailed in the privacy of my own home
long after the funeral was over, with only the hurting eyes
of my husband to behold me—a kind of holding
that was never meant to be done alone.

I imagine that if killer whales were not endangered,
Tahlequah would have swam those seventeen days
with a grand procession of many other glistening,
black and white giants all across the ocean.
Or perhaps she swam for one thousand miles
to personify the loneliness of her grief
in a world spiraling toward oblivion.

And our savagery for not swimming alongside her;
for taking pictures, for watching her exquisite ceremony
on our little screens as if it were pure entertainment,
as if that couldn't be any one of us, carrying our dead
children out into the dark and emptied streets.

THE BREAKDOWN

"It is our deep grief that the village did not appear." - Frances Weller

New Mothers walk around with stunned looks on their haggard faces, every muscle and mouth gasping from the sheer weight of what used to be carried, sown, and cultivated by an entire village. Oh sure, the people came, but only in the beginning, only when her body was laid out in bed, when friends and neighbors filled the fridge with comforting food (that was sometimes too rich to eat) and occasionally did a load of laundry. But they always left as quickly as they arrived, rushing off to tend to their own untenable lives, their nuclear homes. It's true, everyone is stretched beyond what is reasonable in order to maintain a way of life that was never meant to thrive. Although, one of the places you can see the insanity of this arrangement most is on the faces of new Mothers (you can also see it in their aching backs, the crying out of their pelvic floors, racing hearts, anxious minds, depressed souls, and sleep patterns that may never return to normal).

Those early days were lovely, when some distant memory rose up in the blood of that new Mother's community, and so, they leaned in. But where were they in the middle of the night when she and her baby were sobbing and scared? Where were they when she was desperate for sleep or space or comfort, when her marriage began to crumble because two people were not made to lift a little life into the world on their own, or much later on as her baby grew to be fat and beautiful, and her hands, wrists, arms, neck, back hurt so badly from all the holding, which she had to keep on doing because no one else was there, when her body began to break down because it was the only body that this child depended upon to survive, where were they?

One day, I was in a store with my baby when an older man walked over to say hello and boast about his four wonderful grandchildren. I remarked that he must be quite busy, what with chasing all those young ones around. "Busy? Oh no, not me!" he declared. "My daughter is the one who is busy. I am retired. I don't have to do any work at all." And then I stopped wondering where they all went, for he said it so plainly, as if everyone else understood this unfortunate piece of reality but me. The responsibility of a child falls squarely onto the shoulders of their Mothers, no village required. I went home that day and wept.

RAGE/THE RIVER

One day, you cried so hard
you turned into a river—
your body shook

and your shaking became
the thunder thundering over
that river, anger twisted in you
with its sharp edges, with its lightning
striking trees along the banks of the river

with its electrical currents
traveling down into the Earth
then back up and out again

through the breath of every being nearby
and you watched their fear as they exhaled
the enormity of you. You never knew
you could feel so intently, but
you can and you do.

You never knew it could be like this,
no one told you it would be like this.
They did not prepare you for the river.

What you needed was eclipsed by silences
and if not silences, then platitudes.

Language was the sister that was stolen
from them, just as it has been stolen from you.

Only two centuries ago our sisters
were locked away for feeling this deeply,
they were called hysterical and worse

for their rage, which was really their wisdom,
their limits, their inability to submit, to be
stretched until they were broken in two.

That was only eight generations ago, or our
Great Grandmother's Great, Great, Grandmother.
It is close enough for their rage to still rush
through the length of our bodies like wildfire

for the screams and sobs they learned
to swallow, for the silences they padded
around themselves for protection,
the way they went numb, all of it

so that they would not be taken
away from their children.

Or, if they had already been locked up,
their silence became the road by which
they could return. And now, we are

brailing our way along the fallen trees
with their jagged stumps

clinging to the body of the river,
with their scars and burnt flesh

with their silences bending
into something else, into
a kind of redemption.

We are reclaiming our Mother tongues,
we are remembering the breadth of us,
the necessity of anger as a conductor,

as a current that can carry
our aching hearts gently
into a new terrain.

TO BE EMPTIED

Somedays I am a shell of myself, a hollow bone,
a tree struck dumb by lightning yet still improbably
standing. I am a shriveled, old husk rattling in the wind.

Recently, someone ate all of my sweet, fat kernels,
I heard the explosion of nourishment making its way
into that creature's supple body as my body went bare.

I can barely remember what it feels like to be full,
to be un-expectant, to blossom and shimmer.
You could love your life and still know despair

from time to time. You could wish this world was otherwise,
but you would be wishing your life away. You would be
missing the cavern of your days, the way this shell

must be emptied so that a Great Goddess can finally
take up residence in the sanctity of your bones, so that
She can tell the story of your magnificent undoing.

SO I BAKED AS IF MY LIFE DEPENDED UPON IT

And he said, "When things get hard
bake a batch of cinnamon rolls."

It's the only piece of parenting advice
I can remember, even as my husband
and I received legions more in those
final, delirious weeks of pregnancy.

And it came from a neighbor I hardly know,
who learned it from his Grandmother/the woman
who raised him, so I took the instruction seriously.

At first, I only made cinnamon rolls on the weekends.
They had big globs of coconut frosting on top and
we would invite friends over to help us eat them
straight out of the oven while our baby nursed,
slept, or fussed. But it didn't take long to realize

that hard days came easy, so I baked them mid-week
too and without much effort my husband and I would
devour the entire batch. Eventually, our hunger vaulted
in different directions so I began baking other things—
mostly to rescue myself from the abyss, but sometimes

it was purely for pleasure, purely to stand in the presence
of beauty again, to reimagine myself as an alchemist, as one
who knows how to transform our burdens into sustenance.

Lemon sugar cookies with lavender frosting,
double dark chocolate zucchini bread, blueberry
almond crumb cake, cherry frangipane tart,

peanut butter stuffed brownies, oatmeal raisin
cookies, savory pot pies, sprouted grain bread.

"You can try to eat everything that you bake yourself
but it isn't pretty," said my friend Sally, also a baker.
It's not so much that I wanted our lives to be pretty,
more like succulent, more like something that can
always be shared. So, we started throwing parties

even when we were not sleeping, when we could not tell
our right foot from our left, we opened up our home because
we understood that hospitality was the suitor to our hardships.

And I spent full days in the kitchen being a magician—
it kept me from sliding out of this world. As our baby grew,
she began to sit on the counter beside me, tasting the batter,
stirring the wet ingredients into the dry, spilling flour everywhere.

Now, she is learning how to crack eggs on the side of the bowl,
even as shells always get inside and I have to fish them out, I let her,

even as our days are still hard, the smell of vanilla
fills the house and somehow we are made whole again.
As we wait for the cake to rise, as we call our people
to gather round the table, to share in this kindness,
somehow the hard places inside of me soften,

they become like dough, like the leavening
agent to a life born of succulence.

THE ONES WHO MAKE AND
UNMAKE A LIFE

There was once a hunter who fell in love with a deer woman. He followed her tracks for many years, eventually courting her into his heart and home. Her wildness both scared and strengthened him. The deer woman adored the hunter, though their love did not come easy. They had to learn the wooded and sophisticated ways of one another, they had to trace their fingers along the sorrows each of them carried for the worlds they had given up in order to be together.

They were married in the high mountains over several crisp and mysterious days, when the surrounding aspens flushed orange and gold. No one had seen such a ceremony before, or if they had, it wasn't for a very long time. The hunter and deer woman's shared life was spoken into being by all of their people, for better or for worse. They emerged tender-hearted and even more whole than they had been before, ready to turn outward, ready to let the world stand in the center of their love.

One day the deer woman became pregnant. She continued to walk the woods with her swift gait as her belly swelled and their stories deepened. She laid on the Earth every morning as a ritual, as the most trustworthy thing she knew how to do for growing the child inside of her. The hunter designed and built a hearth in their home with the help of a friend. It was what he knew how to do—to make a welcoming place for fire, for a beating heart inside of the life they were being dreamt into.

When the child finally arrived, she was born of their unconventional love, she was from them, but not of them. She was her own myth, conjured by the nobility of every other plant, rock, animal, and human who had walked, prowled, soared, and sang before them. She was a lion cub, furry and fierce. A warrior girl, beautiful and brave. They recognized her immediately.

The hunter, deer woman, and lion cub lived with their wolf pup, an unwieldy family who apprenticed themselves to a kind of story they had seldom seen in the civilized world with its speed and endless need for more. They practiced being slow and needing less, they used their hands, made beauty and songs, danced for every reason, opened their home often to feast and toast with friends and neighbors.

And so the story goes. There is no happily ever after because they are real and fallible, still learning and letting go. Because they are shaped by all the other beings that surround them, the ones who make and unmake a life— the snow and sage, the elk, hawk, fox, trees, hills, raspberries, all the Aunties and Uncles of that little lion cub, the Old Ones, the rivers and places across the ocean, the eloquence spoken between those places, the longing that lives in their bones, the guitar and the loom, the sunrise, sunset, Equinox, and Solstice.

And so, if I am to be faithful to their story, then I must tell you the stories of all these other ones too. It looks like we will be here for a long time. Where shall I begin?

SILVER HAIRED BEAUTY

For Mary

There was a time when they told stories about women
such as you—eventually, those stories became legends
and then they shape-shifted into the starlit sky

which every other woman looked to
to navigate the dark and stormy oceans
of her life. They say the way you walk
is water, your footfall like currents

endlessly falling into love
with all that is and will ever be.
They say that everything you touch
turns to beauty, and if not beauty, then power—
the way when rain comes after years of drought
it can both give and take life at once.

They say your voice is magic,
it can speak whole worlds into being.
Its secret wisdom is praise
for the sunrise and moonshine,
the tendrils of memory curling
through landscapes by way
of rivers and springs.

They say when you laugh
the seasons bloom—
when you drum, journey, or cry
the world is remade into something
not so wholly broken, a place
worth loving and dying for.

They say you are brave
and that you were born this way.
Your noble ancestors stitched bravery
into the inner lining of their cells,
they passed their willingness to show up
for the mysteries of living
all the way down
to you.

They say a lot more
about love stories within love stories,
picking up and setting down, un-damming rivers,
and sediment and dreaming and healing wounds
cut into the womb of the Earth with comfrey.

A fiery passion for mullein, milkweed, and
chocolate. Strong and tender, loyal and fierce.
Mother. Daughter. Sister. Auntie. Lover. Queen.

One day I will tell them I know you
and that all of it is true.

THERE ARE WORDS

My body came from the body of a brave woman,
a strong woman, a wise and kind woman.
My flesh is her flesh, my longing
her longing. Which means
I too am a brave woman,

a strong woman, a wise
and kind woman

and surely her granddaughter
who came barreling through my body
carries the grace of my Mother's body,
which means that at one year old
she is already all of these things, too.

They say there are no words
to describe the pain left like a crater
in the hearts of those who are left behind

but surely there are words.
Surely moments such as these
ache to be spoken to
if only we would try.
So let me try.

Sometimes the pain is so real
you can hold it in your hands

you can carry it into bed and when shaken awake
at 2AM from a nightmare that you can't recall
but which will haunt you for the rest of your life,
at least you can know the pain will still be there

like a lover who never leaves,
curled up around your body
and so you curl up around it, too.

When the world turns away,
when it marches on like it always will
to the next seductive horizon

leaving you standing there
in the dust and the tears
and the insistent yearning,
it is the broken-heartedness
that will never abandon you,

that will remind you their life was real.

They existed because you dare to love them still,
because you are brave enough to carry them
into this day, and the next

because you are too strong to look away,
too wise or kind to concern yourself
with any other seduction.

And your heart hurts all the time,
it breaks over and over again
beneath your lovely clothes
so nobody knows or cares.

Yet you still care—

you must never stop caring
lest their lives cease to matter.
You must tell their stories,

speak their names,
dance, weep, sing.

DANCING IN THE KITCHEN

Light picks up the shape of autumn leaves
and makes a kind of music with them,
my body moves to that music
as it hasn't moved in years.

I am not so good at inhabiting joy but
the long lineage braided into my baby's smile—
the way she throws her head back, unabashed
and laughs into the sudden air—is teaching me,
the change of seasons is teaching me

that everything pleasurable in this world
is worth swaying ones hips to.

Most evenings, my daughter and I dance in the kitchen
while dinner sizzles and spits in the oven, while her daddy
drives to us through his great love and longing for home.

I grew up dancing: hours upon hours each week
in the studio, wrapping my body around ballet bars
and throwing my limbs through the air like thunder.
But with pain, and time, and my Mother's decline
I stopped moving entirely, stopped praying

in that sort of way. It had been a decade or more
since I did a pirouette or plié, since I tossed my legs
skyward and rolled around on the floor, since I felt
how the piano and violin ripple through my spine
like a serpent, like the proverbial woman
who never left the garden,

who, after biting hungrily into that blessed apple,
relished the sensation of fragrant juices
dripping down her thighs.

Birthing a daughter reawakened this rapture inside me;
watching her twirl and bounce her strong little body
in shapes and rhythms that are wholly woven
into the cosmology from which she came

has allowed my body to remember,
to reclaim the importance of
courting an unbridled joy.

A LOVE LETTER TO MY DAUGHTER'S AUNTIES

Even as I've learned to hope for nothing, there is you

and you give me hope for this world my daughter
is growing into. Thank you for being the wise and
rooted trees standing around her, throwing shade

on days when the heat makes it too hard to breathe
and a long-limbed dance in moments where movement
is the only way we can say what we really mean.

I am indebted to your wild generosity,
your strength in the hours of my weakness,

your patience and grace when I have
nothing left to offer, you offer.

Bless you for being the forest that feeds
the canticle brilliance of our days,

for reimagining kinship
into a land that breathes.

You are teaching my daughter
how to orient her heart,

what belonging actually means

and you are teaching me
about the kind of woman

I want to be.

SOMETHING ANCIENT

The first autumn of our daughter's life,
my husband shot a deer and an elk,
we were bewildered by our good fortune.

We spent days butchering in the kitchen
while our six month old baby played at our feet,
while friends and neighbors came over to hold her,
play with her, to help wrap the meat, cut the bones,
cradle the heart and liver, sing, tell stories and
shed tears over the two blessed animals/ancestors
that would grant us life for the following year.

I watched the ordinariness of such a thing
as it landed in my daughter's being, how obvious
it was to her that we would participate in the making
of life and death, the offerings, the stripping of hide
from sinew encased flesh, the pungent aroma and
deep red blood on the counter, on her parent's hands
and clothes, the piles of bones, the endless hours of work
and exhaustion, the way grief and gratitude were cousins

chasing one another around the kitchen and falling down
in fits of breathlessness, of wonder, of the truest kind
of ceremony she had ever seen. If we want to eat meat,
this is how it is done, said her tiny, primal body.
If we want to know our humanity, this is also how
it is done. We will not outsource the killing,
we will not pretend death does not exist
when it is the reason we exist.

I saw all of this in the easy way she moved through
those laborious days and I learned something
ancient about my capacity as her Mother.

So, in the second autumn of our daughter's life,
I carried her on my back up and down hills
to the place where my husband knelt
beside the doe he had recently shot—

our friends were standing around the deer's
fallen body too, making offerings and heaving
their sorrow, their praise into the frosty air.

Our daughter watched as her daddy slid his knife
along the length of the doe's soft, brown belly,
as he found a puddle of milk waiting inside,

as dusk settled deeper into that late-November sky,
as he steadied his hands and worked with tears
streaming down his cheeks, as the world stopped
for a time so we could remember our place within it.

And much later on, after we ground the meat,
after we scrubbed the counters and carried the hooves
back out onto the land, after we prayed over those hooves,
after we watched grief and gratitude, those wild cousins,
make a wreckage of our days, we grilled steaks

and sat together at the table, our daughter
eagerly reaching for the plate, her hands so open,
so new, reaching over and over again from the plate
to her mouth, like a ritual, like she understood
what all the sorrow and effort was for.

Like she had seen the body of this animal,
the bones and the blood, like she would not
stop eating until she felt our ancestor
stand up and leap inside of her.

KNEELING DOWN

If you stop pretending that you are somehow
better than your heartbreak, or that you have managed
to get over it quicker than what is wholly possible

in a body forever tenderized by time,
it will begin teaching you things

about how to become a fully fledged human,
it will show you what is truly required to love
and breathe and walk through the corridor
of every ordinary day. Your heartbreak

will tell stories around the winter fires,
it will remember all of the taking and
giving that is braided into the spirit
of any honest life. It will ask you

to stop handing off the impossible weight
of these things to some unassuming other,
it will beg you to begin bearing the weight—

to wear it around your shoulders like a finely woven,
woolen shawl made by the benevolent hands of your
rightful people. It will paint pictures with your tears

it will chisel stone with all the things that are free of fairness
yet still exist in this world and kneel down onto the holy ground,

too. It will stop tolerating your entitlements,
all those simple things, those profound things
you forever take for granted. It will lead you

deeper into your days, it will become a trustworthy frame,
that brokenness—always crooning, always claiming, always
making a place for you to fall heart-first into your wholeness.

MOTHERLINE

The Barbarians were the bearded ones, the heathens, the Indigenous Peoples of Europe. They were the Pagans, Animists, polytheists, artists, bards, warriors, clans of nomadic folk who resisted empire, who lived outside of the cities and danced under the silver or darkened moon, who made offerings to the spirits of place—to the trees, rain, deer, fairies, wells, and elves.

They are the unnamed or blasphemous ones in our history books who were forced to give up their culture, language, and spiritual ways of life by Christian Crusaders; who were shamed, tortured, raped, and killed unless they swore to pray to the one God who sanctioned all of this violence, anyway. They are our ancestors. They are us.

We are the ones who were forced into the cities, away from ritual and land. We are the ones who traded in our life-ways for a foreign faith and savage forgetting. But these sanctified bones kept on singing, they kept on dancing under the starlet sky, except now it looks like shaking, and it is only our dreams that hold the shape of a time when things were otherwise.

THE CURRENT OF OUR DIVISIONS

Maybe division and distance
and blame is all we know,
maybe it's all we're capable of

as people who left the bones
of our peoples behind

in all those deserted places
so far away across the sea.
Maybe it's easier this way,

to keep recreating the past
with its multitude of sorrows
and misunderstandings—

maybe the patterns are engrained
in us, so tattooed onto the topographical
map of our bodies and psyches

that we can no longer discern
the sorrows, which have become
just another deserted thing.

Maybe we are carried along
by the current of our divisions,
by the wounds of our people
that were never permitted to heal.

My Mother did not speak to her Mother
for thirty years, not even a word before she died.
Which means I grew into the world without
a Maternal Grandmother, that I will forever

have a fissure in my heart the shape
and breadth of a falling star.

It also means that my Grandmother
is still alive, sitting alone in her high rise
apartment in Denver with fake jewels
on every single finger. I visited her there
a few times—the first was at the end
of my Mother's life. I was the one

to inform this eighty-two year old woman
that her estranged daughter was about to die.
I was the one to look into her anesthetized eyes,
to witness the way she would not cry.

Then, I visited her again—
several months after my Mother's body
had been laid into the Earth. I could not stop crying,
I could not keep it together (though she asked me to)
and she refused to shed a single, shining tear.

But she did request a ride to Target
on that first visit so she could return
a few things, and on the last visit
she asked for help with fixing her TV.

Maybe our wounds have been
toughened into scar tissue
and fortified by time.

Maybe tears are now trapped
inside our slowly dying hearts,

maybe they have been replaced
by distraction and consumption,

maybe the only way
we can continue breathing
is to keep handing over our humanity

to all of the shadows that benefit
from our divisions, our pain,

our inability to heal.

KEEPER OF ALL THINGS

When I close my eyes
I see my Mother's hands,

slender and strong, I see
the way her purple veins swell
like many rivers flowing.

I trace my fingers along
her rivers and I overhear
the many stories of her life.

When I open my eyes and look
at my hands, I see her hands
shapeshifting into mine.

When I hold my baby
I see her holding her baby,

the way her hands
spread like talons

to support my
growing body,

how she traces her fingers
along my brow and into
my golden hair—time
is an unbroken animal,

it is the keeper of all things,
bending it's head to drink

from every river
we can and cannot see.

MOTHER NIGHT

You are so full of life.

You are fertile with the dancing body,
the dreaming body, with quiet visions
waiting to be carried into the shouting

light of day. You are the lover of all things
disowned by the day world—our deliverance
from productivity and the incessant need to be seen.
You do not claim certainty as a way toward anything

in fact, you uphold the mysteries of creation
as they are continually unmade and made again
inside the songs you sing to every star and
beating heart curled up against the wild shape
of your achingly beautiful breast. I love you

and I fear you
for I can never quite
find rest inside of you.
You rise and sway and
turn and incite magic

into every cell of my trembling being,
a being who was made in the image
of her roaring Mother. You bend me

toward poetry and prophecy,
you break me into something
I didn't know I was meant to be.

If only I could write or make beauty
from sun down to sun up in your dark,
holy arms and then give my exhausted bones
over to sleep for the duration of the day—
I would be a different creature entirely,
not so tortured by my desperation.

I would be a nightingale, a sorceress,
a dancing woman who knows
her place beside the exalted moon,
ever changing, ever worthy of praise.

SPILLING FORTH

"And it is decided matter is dead." —Susan Griffin

But you are not dead, are you
Mother? Even when your child cries
and you cry and no one comes to help you,
even when you have been home alone for days,
when you have understood that madness is not
a distant land but a rosebush that lives inside of you.
Or, when you have been working outside of the house
all week and so can not bend down to bury your nose
into your child's hair, to breathe in the scent of your
creative power whenever the impulse arises,
when you are too tired to lift your hands
toward all the things that once stirred you
into the sweetest kind of motion.

Yet somehow you keep on laboring and soothing,
cooking and carrying way beyond your capacity
to do these things, which is when you realize
you are an endless reservoir of giving
and giving and giving—and in that moment
you understand a second thing, which is that
even though they told you selflessness
is what you should aspire to, in the end,
it would be the thing that would crush you.
It would take your heart into its hands
and squeeze so tightly that you
would not be able to scream.

Because isn't it true, a reservoir is always a river
that has been damned and diverted, a glistening body
of water utterly prevented from flowing in the direction
of her longing? And even then, Mother, when all is lost,
including the shape of your name and fading desires,
your heart still beats, it still ticks off every second
of every day like a bomb waiting to blow apart
the walls that keep your life from spilling forth.

WE STOPPED TRYING

I brought a meal to a new family recently.
I sat with the Mother as she nursed her newborn
with wild eyes, like they had been gutted
and replaced by Saturn's many moons.

"How do you get used to it?" she asked,
her moons glowing, orbiting the room.

Her question penetrated the air around us,
the silence in her house felt deafening.
We were the only two women there that day

and somehow I already knew what she
was asking, what *it* was, but she went on,
"Somedays I just find myself feeling so lonely."

I had only been a Mother for a year and a half
longer than she had, so my response was short,
"You do not." And the silence deepened,

it engulfed us, we were swimming in it,
so for a moment we swam together,
we kept treading water, we let go

of needing to pretend
that this way of Mothering
was normal, when it is not so.

And then we stopped trying to
acclimate to such an abnormal thing,
we decided to be brokenhearted instead—

to let our bones have their memories,
how we were always meant to be braided
into the stream of many generations,

of the old and the young helping to track,
feed, love, and plead with the Gods

for the rain to keep on coming,
for the sun and the stars to not
lose sight of us, for our lives
to be a gesture of their praise.

So we sat there looking over our shoulders,
squinting our eyes into the silence and
trying to catch a glimpse of our own Mothers,

of our Aunties and Grandmothers—the ones who
knew nurturance to be the most noble endeavor,
who knew how to teach us all of the things
we were not born knowing how to do.

And something in that silence
squinted back at us, too.

THE HUNT

There are three baby foxes in our neighborhood,
their den is beneath a big, specked boulder
in our neighbor's yard, they play in the grass
and sun on surrounding rocks as their Mother
hunts for food. I have seen her hunting—

her plush fur a streak of fire in the feracious green,
her attentive eyes hungering for a future her children
have not been promised. This hunt is their promise.

I watch her stealth movements, how precisely she
stops, still as stone, her ears fully alive, listening
and I feel my body listening, hunting, too.

I am crouching down in the grass beside her,
our shoulders rise like boulders as one leg lifts and
the other leg lowers, as pure desire carries us forward.
Our bodies know no other strength, no other devotion.

We must leave our babies from time to time
in order to feed them, in order to be creatures
of consequence in this world. But leaving
becomes our prayer for a full bodied return.

TO KNOW SWEETNESS

This is the year I am determined to taste a pear
from our single fruiting tree. Every other year
the magpies and rock squirrels have claimed them all,
every single one when they were still too small
to be sweet, and besides, hard as rocks.

Survivorship is not a concept for these tenacious creatures,
it is a God, a way of knowing the rigors of this world.

I am determined this year not because I feel entitled
to the pear's delicate, speckled flesh; not even because
I have spent countless evenings kneeling at the tree's feet,
proffering rainwater that had been collected from our roof—
evenings when my own feet ache from standing in the kitchen
with a baby on my hip while cobbling together dinner,
while my back stiffens then screams for some sort of relief.

Nor because I so often peel myself from the couch
once my baby is asleep to go out and water,
to peer up into the pear's holy branches
to see if any fruit is left hanging

peering up even when my eyes will barely open.
No, none of this vindicates my determination.
This deep-seated need to know sweetness
is sung from the same breeze that wraps herself
ever so gently around my own heavy limbs,
rarely reaching skyward except for in my dreams.

The sun rays which are ripening both me
and every one of those green, glistening jewels
into something tender-skinned and heart-shaped,
into a living thing worthy of being savored.

The real reason is because I have heard the tree
laughing. I have so often watched her dancing
beneath each resplendent phase of the moon,
I have beheld her pure joy even while carrying
all of those hefty, stone fruit children.
I have seen her devotion to live
and love this world, still.

My body needs to ingest
what she is carrying

to feed from that generosity,
to know that kind of improbable joy
and then fling it back to every other
survivor of this harsh world

as a beacon, as a ballad,
as a balm for all that ails us.

TO *REALLY* KNOW SWEETNESS

For Dave and Renée

I am told that some farmers sleep in their orchards with shotguns
precisely at the moment their fruit trees begin to ripen, precisely
as all the other creatures begin hankering after late summer's
sweetness, too. Aren't madness and love sometimes the same thing?

I am not a farmer, but I do know longing. I often wear it around my neck
like a garland, fingering the flowers and smelling their fragrance
until I am intoxicated by life's unfurling, until my whole body is buzzing
and I can no longer find the night-road which leads every weary heart to sleep.

And so, when finally all the mountain creatures came to claim our pears,
when they graciously left one glistening jewel still hanging, I climbed
up into the tree to retrieve it while my dog and daughter stood on the ground
watching. I held this precious being in my hands, hands which every day are aging,

the tears in my eyes were joyful and real. I carried that single piece
of speckled fruit back into the house, while balancing my baby
again on my hip and trying to explain to her why the pear
was still not ripe, why we would need to wait a bit longer
to sink our hearts and teeth into its tender flesh.

So I placed the pear in our fruit basket, the one I wove
long before becoming pregnant, before giving my life over
to the laborious feat of growing our future. And a week later
when the pear had finally softened, when it was hours away
from turning mealy, when I had picked up some seasonal illness
and my sinuses were so congested that I could not smell or taste a thing,
when I was dragging myself through my days because a sick Mother

is the crucible of our current poverties,
of how truly untenable it is to parent
without a proper village—

I slowly, ceremonially ran a knife through the pear's skin.
I cut pieces for myself and my ever-hungry-daughter,
I brought one of those pieces to my lips
though I could not taste it.

The tragedy, even the cruelty of spending
so many months longing for this very moment
only to have my tastebuds decisively deadened
and yet, I could not possibly feel sorry for myself
because the pear's juices were spilling
down my daughter's smiling chin.

She was laughing, she was making sounds of delight
and raising her little hands into the air for more.
I do not believe in martyrdom, but I do believe
in sweetness seeping from the pores of that
which we are lucky enough to see. I believe

that true, initiated adults
might not live to taste the fruits
of their labors, yet they still labor

on behalf of the next generation. I believe
in the sanctity of taking less, so much less

from the Earth so that future ones can actually
have a place to come into and love and be held by,
to become fully human in and for. I believe in relishing

all of these blessed moments and not pining after
ones that are yet to come, that may never come.

I believe that longing can be
a sensuous thing of the present,
it can be a body that calls us home.

SO I SCRUB

In the evening, when the sun begins his noble descent behind the hills and the bright air breathes her song back into the Earth, I go outside to take the diapers down from the clothesline after hanging all day in the mountain wind like tattered prayer flags. Dinner is in the oven and I am tired. My back hurts and I have gone another day without drinking enough water. My brittle fingers finger the clothespins and for a moment we recognize our need to hold onto one another—our stiffness has purpose when pinned together.

Eventually, after all has been gathered and I turn back for the oven-warmed-house, an owl hoots in the shadowy forest, reminding me that I too am a cup of wilderness. Although, sometimes this awareness is hard to hold onto when I spend so many hours inside, the scent of domesticity clinging to my hair, my clothes.

And the amount of time that my body is folded over the toilet scrubbing diapers might seem ungodly by today's standards, when convenience is all the rage. Sometimes, I fantasize about how much easier things would be if I could simply throw a soiled diaper away—I think of other parents who do this a dozen times a day, who likely are not as intimate with smells and sights that provoke gagging and profanity, and I wonder what else they must be doing with their freed-up time? Even still, I continue to bow over the toilet bowl and scrub shit. It's not that I have lost my mind (although sometimes this is true, but I always seem to find it again), it's because I know that convenience comes at an incredibly high cost, that in reality, there is no away.

What a person knows, they can not un-know, for example: disposable diapers produce millions of tons of toxic waste per year, many end up floating in our oceans, and the ones that do manage to stay in the overflowing garbage dumps take at least five centuries to decompose. Thankfully, I am also reminded that 'domestic', at it's root, was not the slandered term it has become today. I know it's true meaning, which is to tend to the soul of a home.

So, I scrub as a Mother whose parallel work is to tend to the soul of this world. I scrub for my daughter, but also for all of the young ones who are set to inherit a precious and seriously mistreated planet. I scrub because I'm in love with their true Mother—the one they will return to in the end, this breathing and achingly beautiful Earth I have vowed to honor, to lay bare Her good name like a prayer waving in the wind.

THE PROMISED LAND

Did you know there is an island of trash twice the size of Texas,
or three times the size of France, floating in the Pacific Ocean?

If water is life, and surely the ocean is Mother of us all,
then what does this say about the way we humans treat our
sustainer, our lover and beauty-maker, joy-bringer and
great luminous body from which we once emerged
to become air breathers, star-gazers, basket-weavers,

hunters and huntresses, village-tenders, slingers of magic,
poetry, prayer, compassion, and rage? What does this say

about our ability to transpose plastics into Gods
and feed them ceaselessly to this Great Goddess
whose belly is nauseous and bulging from our
careless consumption? What does it say

that even upon knowing the island exists, and
that every day it grows bigger, we will keep on
consuming? That we've so thoroughly absorbed
the belief of an entirely separate land hovering
above this one, disconnected from the dirt

and salt and silky animal bodies ingesting our trash,
a land gilded in gold and polished to perfection—

that wrecking our current home, this oceanic wonder
soaring through space, has become a common practice
even encouraged, since there will be another home

pious and waiting for us in the next life
no matter how much we buy and throw away
in this one. It's a story that has been dispersed
and ingrained so deeply that we abide by it

even if we are not believers. It is the besotted waters
from which we collectively drink and bathe, jet set,
surf, and swim. If you knew in your bones that the Earth
was the promised land, wouldn't you act differently?

Perhaps you tried for awhile, a long while,
but the rampant defilement drove you mad
or forced you to collapse into apathy.
After all, the energy of a mass swarm of fish
is always stronger than a few lone travelers.

IMAGINING WORLDS LESS BROKEN THAN THIS ONE

Yesterday there was another school shooting. 3 children were killed. There have been dozens of school shootings since my daughter was born. It is unfathomable, and yet, not entirely surprising given the way this country was formed, given that we are living in the ghosted lands of fathomless transgression—gentle and sane citizens do not descend from that kind of beginning.

In less than 2 years, 47 children have been killed in and around their desks with books opened to pages that they will never get to finish. In a few months my daughter will be 2 years old and I do not know how to talk to her about this world.

Right now she is sitting on the couch with books scattered around her. She is studying pictures, lingering over the places where those children's lives ended. She is running her chubby little fingers across the pages and imagining worlds less broken than this one. She is quiet and focused, her round cheeks are resting on her rising chest and I am cherishing her profile from the kitchen while cleaning the breakfast dishes and thinking about all of the parents who are getting their children ready for school. I am thinking about their fear, their grief. Our grief.

I remember the way my Mother ran to me from across the parking lot after I had been in lockdown at a middle school just a few miles away from Columbine. I remember the look in her eyes as she ran—a desperate relief, a howling pain, a terror, a Mother's worst nightmare spared this time but what about the next time, and so she ran as though she was running from a monster, running toward her beating heart standing there outside of her chest in the oppressive light of that warm spring day.

I remember the way she sobbed when she held me, the way she tried to pull me back inside of her body. My Mother cried for weeks after that, her tears became a river that carried those 12 murdered teenagers to wherever they were meant to go next, the currents were swift and achingly kind. I didn't know it then, but at 13 years old I was learning, in my Mother's grief, what Mothering meant—that love does not begin and end with your own children, it is the very air and soil and sunlight that sustains our broken world even in its most unforgivable brokenness.

AN OPENED WING

Motherhood has made me too literal:
count the months, then the days and
of course, always the hours. Remember
to breathe, to sit down while eating,
stop here, do not stop over there.

I am choking on straight lines even as
my daughter spins in circles around me—
I hold the center while my center comes undone,
lest we both get lost in some ruinous storm or metaphor.

I have written, no, clawed through, too many clichés
and I have thrown too many terrible poems away
because Motherhood is not a cliché, it is a shoreline,
an opened wing holding both the land and the sea.

A BODY CAUGHT ON FIRE

If I could play any instrument
(and I've never played any instrument,
I mean *really* played, like the shape of the
music maker itself beginning to shape shift
in your hands, like a kind of dancing,

like a body caught on fire)
it would most certainly be
the saxophone.

Many of my friends' ears are not so keen
on jazz, the sound of this unmistakable,
wind-driven instrument in particular—
too loud, too brazen, too unwilling
to blend into the background
of any blessed tune.

But I love that about the sax,
I hear the sound and swoon.
How could anything be both
sharp and smooth? Even sexy,
and unapologetically owning
every ounce of itself all the way
down to the last lingering note

suspended in the air like a torch,
like the moon with her silver smile
and sultriness, with her way of dazzling
every night creature into fits of wonder.

Forget wanting to play the sax,
I want to *be* the sax—so like that,
so unafraid of inhabiting my own soul.

BE LIKE THE BLUEBELLS

Take the hands you have so inadequately learned to love
and bless this world with your beauty-making. Holding back
what is yours to give has never been a viable option,
though you chose it, over and again. But now

as you watch the land burning, as you feel
the thirst and hunger and pleading of this world
rolling through your cells like thunder,

you know that everything from this moment onward
must change. You know you must be like the bluebells
returning in spring, the way they blossom without inhibition,
the way they give all of their nectar to the bees' holy mouths,

to the pollination of our futures—how they drop each and
every one of their lovely petals down onto the rising Earth
like presents or prayers, blue laid gently over brown and
green. How without accolade, they go on blessing
this world up to, and even beyond, their gentle deaths.

GRIEF'S LESSER-KNOWN LONGING

For Sage

Two Mothers sit at a table weaving baskets:
the first one's daughter died before taking her first
breath, the second one's daughter is upstairs taking a nap.

The Mothers soak the reed in water and wait
until the pieces are malleable. Then, they plunge
their hands—hands which have held both life and
death—into the cool bath. They pull one piece

out at a time, dripping, they lay the long and now
limber reed on the table. Over and under, under and
over they layer the strands, their fingers following

ancestral pathways, their bodies falling into rhythm,
into the understanding of grief's lesser-known longing—
to be transformed into something that is both beautiful

and useful. There is no difference between the love
that these two Mothers have for their daughters,
how the soaked reed guides their wet fingers,
the way their baskets speak to them and they listen,

how they help to shape the strands into something
different than what they were before, and gently,
rhythmically the Mothers are reshaped, too.

They tell stories while they work, over and under,
under and over, and their words are woven into a vessel
you can see and hold. You can turn it around in your own hands,
take it out to the garden and fill it with herbs or tomatoes,
you can imagine a baby sleeping inside of it's woven body,

and the Mother that birthed that baby—you can see
her profound strength, you can hear her wisdom
in the elegance of the weave, and you can know
that magic does exist, how all of life depends upon it.

COILING

Love is the pitcher that we fill to pour
over the garden, it is the water

hydrating the parched soil and making
the plants sing. It is the singing

the way it enters our throats when we eat
the greens, the grapes, the raspberries

and coils back out in unexpected ways.
It is the coiling, the real reason

we keep rising each morning
to stare into the face of creation,

to say, "I am your consort,
turn my heart into compost,

into an emissary of nourishment,
a seed that both feeds and is fed by

the promise of decay."

THE EGG THAT DIDN'T RELEASE

Sometimes poetry is disguised as science, for example,
we now know that all the eggs we will ever have
are formed in our ovaries while we are still inside
of our Mother's wombs. This gives me solace

particularly on the days I wish my daughter
could have met my Mother, when my wishing
becomes a world that hurts, when I worry about

the hole that my daughter is carrying around in her heart,
how nothing can fill the emptied space of a Maternal
Grandmother. Thankfully, this science/poetry reminds me

that my daughter was once the seed of a dream in her
Grandmother's cosmic body, that they have known the
shape of each other's lives since the beginning of time.

Today, my midwife calls to say the results are in
from the pelvic ultrasound, to say there is a cyst
the size of two limes on my left ovary.

My daughter is sitting on the counter watching
my face as I receive the news, her eyes say
"Tell me you're ok, Mama." And my eyes say,
"I don't know if I'm ok." And we stay there

in that unknowing, even though it feels hard to stay.
The first time my daughter tasted a lime, I watched her face
as it puckered with surprise, then slowly unfolded into something

I could not name. She continued to suck the fruit
until it was a shriveled thing, her sucking taught her
this world cannot always be sweet.

I wish I would have stayed in the unknown
with my Mother for awhile longer, so determined
as I was to know if she was ok or if death was
upon her, there was nothing in between. No gray,

or in this case green, like the limes
that have grown so quietly inside of me.

AS IF

I will never forget the first time I witnessed
my daughter beholding my naked body—
the first woman's body she had ever fully seen,
a thing of pure beauty held in her newly born eyes.

She was a few months old, laying on top of a sheepskin
in the bathroom and playing with her tiny hands while I bathed.
When I stepped out of the shower, it was as if all the stars in the sky
had fallen at once and landed in the basin of her beaming face.

Her wide, toothless smile contained every constellation,
named and unnamed, as her eyes tripled in size to behold
the soft belly that grew her, the shapely thighs that granted her
not-yet-mobile legs movement, the discolored nipples
and swollen breasts that nourished her, all the scars
and warrior markings that made me her Mother.

It was as if she was staring into the face of the divine,
as if she had yet to absorb that rotten and pervasive script
which tells us we are supposed to hate our bodies,
mistrust our bodies, deprive our bodies—

be in the constant pursuit of changing our bodies,
prevent our bodies from aging/gaining wisdom,
undergo the knife or needle or laser to brutalize
our bodies, make our bodies smaller and
smaller until they are no longer there.

Three weeks after I gave birth, my stepmom asked me
when I was planning to lose my belly fat, as if this
were the most important thing I should be worried about
in that dizzying moment instead of learning how to care

for my new baby, as if it should always be the most
important thing I ought to be worried about
instead of learning how to care for an aching world,

as if it were her place to comment on my body,
as if it is ever anyone's place to comment
on someone else's body.

It wasn't my stepmom, not really; it was the script
speaking through her. And although I knew it was
that rotten thing, even my knowing could not save me.

I burned with contempt and self-consciousness,
I felt diminished and robbed of that precious space
a woman enters into after bearing life from her womb,
where she is both entirely embodied and something
so much more vast than a single body can endure.

So, when the weight did drop off in shards because
breastfeeding turned me into an emptied vessel,
because the sleepless nights sucked me dry as bone
and so, I became bone—people kept emphatically remarking
on how it looked like I had never even been pregnant,
as if this was supposed to be a compliment, as if I should
want to look like a maiden when, in fact, I am a Mother.

The truth is, I missed my belly when it was gone—
the way it held the cosmos, the very origin of life—
which seems hard to believe within a script

that shames us for taking up space
but I will tell you, I missed the space.

And now, at two years old, my daughter's face still shines
when she sees the wondrous body that birthed her, she smiles
and points out all of the holy places illuminating my flesh.

Through her eyes I see myself as we were always meant
to see ourselves—a wild revelation, an exquisite miracle—

just as she is, as you are, and your children, too.

FOREST FIRES

The first evacuation notice came three days after finding out that I was newly pregnant. Flames danced on the distant hillside while we packed up our house. I focused my hands on wrapping my Mother's pottery in blankets, I focused my mind on gently laying each wrapped package in the car. I threw my heart into the preservation of beauty, culture, family, anything to keep myself from thinking about the world burning away. Then we fled—like all our displaced peoples since the beginning of time—and through our fleeing a future one was being made.

The second evacuation notice came when our daughter was a few months old. We were in town when I got the call from a neighbor. I nearly had a panic attack. I'd never had a panic attack before, so there was nothing to compare it to, but breathing felt far away. I stood on the street, holding my baby against my trembling chest while trying to remember how to pull air inside of my body. There was no pottery, no soft blankets, nothing else to focus my hands or mind on, only the calamity of a world in which I brought this child into. No one can say I did not know, I knew.

The third notice came several months later. We were home, our daughter already asleep for the night as fires blazed in the forests nearby. When the alert signaled that we should start preparing to leave, fear and overwhelm besieged me. Like a stunned deer, I sat in the dark of our house, completely unable to move. There was no preservation of beauty then, no possibility of gently wrapping anything—we were adrift in the consequences of a society addicted to destruction and I was as bare as I had ever been. As I will ever be.

THE STRANGE TUNE OF MODERNITY/POSTPARTUM ANXIETY

"It is no measure of health to be well adjusted
to a profoundly sick society." –Jiddu Krishnamurti

At night I lay awake, my body buzzing. It's like electricity is moving through me. I cannot make it stop, for all the things I've tried, it will not stop. My heart thrashes into my rib cage like a caged animal, like she has fists and she wants out, like she wants to walk around this world and see things for herself. Night after night she thrashes, for weeks and months on end until I entirely forget what sleep is, until buzzing/thrashing/the strange tune of modernity becomes the only song inside of me.

Eventually, I am sent in for an electrocardiogram to make sure my heart is alright. When I show up for the appointment, I am struck by how many people are sitting in the waiting room, by how many troubled hearts are palpitating alongside my own—though we do not look one other in the eyes, we do not acknowledge the crisis after crisis in the news, how the skies are smoky again, we are told not to go outside and in the same breath we are told that everything will be alright. So we sit stooped over our thrashing hearts, spooked by the strangeness of the seasons, by our inability to reach out our hands and hold one another, to set this world into a different kind of motion.

When the nurse calls me back to record the waves in my chest, I follow him like an anxious animal emerging from the burning forests—all I can think about is water. Thankfully, he is familiar with the kind of animal that I am, having seen us all day long for weeks and months on end, he works with a kind of tenderness I am not prepared for, a swiftness that lets me breathe. Then, he shows me the sonic image of my heart—dark red lines on white and green paper, lines that look like the scales of music, like jagged mountains punctuated by the seriousness of flat footed valleys, and I want to walk across them, to feel the way my body echoes the rhythmic terrain of the Earth.

When the doctor comes in to look at my music scales, he smiles with kind eyes and tells me that my heart is perfectly healthy. My husband says maybe it is just too big, maybe it feels crammed inside of my small chest. I don't doubt that both my doctor and husband are correct, but what they can not see nor measure is precisely how many times my heart has been broken open.

I know there are chasms wrong with the way we are living now, I know my body is expressing the trembling sorrows of these times. I know Mothers' feet grow gnarled roots that reach deep into the heart of the Earth and so we become the trunks that rise up from those tremors, we become the most trustworthy way of discerning the health or dis-ease of the world that our children will one day inherit.

There are so many Mothers who tell me they can not sleep at night from the buzzing and thrashing, from the terrifying thoughts they have about being alone with their babies, from the improbability of their children's futures. But they always say these things in whispers because everyone knows the ramifications of speaking loudly. Everyone knows it is far easier to medicate the Mothers, to desensitize and silence them instead of trying to change the culture.

A PORTRAIT OF COHERENCE

Sometimes you dream of being absorbed back
into the Earth, of laying your tired bones down

the roots of the oldest trees holding you and you
do not need to hold anything yourself. You dream

of going to a place where no one needs you,
no one calls out your name and it is quiet,

breathtakingly quiet. You can hear yourself breathe,
for the first time in a long time you watch your mind

reassemble itself into a portrait of coherence,
you follow each thought to the very end

those unbroken endings sprout
into a field the size of your body—

a place where beginnings are made.
And you behold each sprout

reaching their tendrils into the patient air,
the way they tremble and whisper,

you overhear your life in their words
and you see your image rising up,

reclaiming herself.
You rise up to meet her.

SONGS OF REMEMBRANCE

Each day we must choose what we give our attention to,
otherwise we would be decimated by all the losses—
by all the fury and winged bodies vanishing from this planet

along with our connection to the particular cosmologies
of our peoples, to their myths and languages, to their
way of caring for the seeds of each new generation.
Which is why we rely on theories and experts
to tell us how to raise our children,
to further our severance

from the wisdom that was sewn into our cells
long before conception, cells that were beckoned forth
from each speck of dust and pollen descending toward the Earth,
from the prayers our ancestors made to those tiny, air-born bodies

prayers that enabled life to keep on living,
prayers that are still fanning out from
the very shores or inland valleys
where they were originally spoken.

I will tell you, Mother, your body is wise
and strong, you would not have survived
the Underworld Journey if this were not true.

You would not keep on surviving
all the heartbreaks of being human,
the disappointments and disorientations,
the extreme lack of sleep and support

surely, if you were weak or daft or inconsequential,
if your wellness was not inherent to the wellness

of this planet. You are the courage and heft
of a thousand generations standing at your back,

kneeling in your blood, singing songs
of remembrance into every cell and tissue,
each drop of milk and sweat and tears

offered as a libation to the Earth
and into the opened mouths of Her babies
for whom your ancestors dream.

POST SCRIPT

Here is the thing I saved for the very end, which I should have told you at the beginning: ceremony always proceeds celebration. But you already knew that, didn't you? You grew life in the cosmic waters of your womb, a ceremonial thing in and of itself. Then, that life traveled through your extraordinary body to become an air breather, to cry, bleed, laugh, love, and dream.

Recently, another Mother told me that since having babies, nothing feels sacred anymore. She told me this while nursing her son, his face so fully turned toward her naked breast that it was as if he had been absorbed into the very origin of sacredness—his tiny mouth working exceptionally hard to send sounds of suckling all throughout the tousled room, six months of life flourishing and feasting upon the nectar from which ceremony is made. The mundane, when handed to us so openly, so without warning or ribbons, is all we've ever had. Perhaps then, it is what this life is for.

Your cooking and cleaning, your tiredness, your longing, your laying down and getting up, your breathing and boredom, your curling into the fetal position when there is never enough time to stay there, your unwashed hair, your hunger, your despair, your awe and resilience, your ancestors whispering words of wisdom and encouragement into your lonesome cells, your body remembering the way back to herself over and again, your nipples, thighs, belly, eyes, hands, and holy heartbeat which sung your children into this world and whose rhythm will orchestrate the maturation of their days—isn't all of this folded into the flowering ceremony that has become your life?

ACKNOWLEDGMENTS

I am grateful to the editors of the following publications where versions of these poems first appeared:

SHE On The Tip of Her Tongue: "Birth Story"

Dawn Songs: A Birdwatcher's Field Guide to the Poetics of Migration edited by Jamie K. Reaser and J. Drew Lanham (Talking Waters Press, 2023): "Mother Canada Goose"

Deep Times: A Journal of the Work that Reconnects: "The Progeny of Love"

Wounded Feminine: Grieving with Goddess edited by Claire Dorey, Pat Daly and Trista Hendren (Girl God Books, 2024): "There Are Words"

Clarion Poetry Magazine: "Birth Story," "Dancing in the Kitchen," and "A Body Caught on Fire"

About the Author

April Tierney is a poet, activist, craftswoman, mother, and lover of stories. She is the author of four full length collections of poetry, including *Memory Keeper* (Wayfarer Books, 2022) and a contributor to several anthologies. Her work has been featured in *Orion, Deep Times: A Journal of the Work that Reconnects, Clarion Poetry Magazine, Real Ground Journal,* and *Wayfarer Magazine,* among others. April lives along the foothills of the Colorado Rocky Mountains with her family. To learn more visit www.apriltierney.com.

WAYFARER

BASED IN THE PIONEER VALLEY, MASS.

At Wayfarer Books we believe poetry is the language of the earth. We believe words—shaped like rivers through wild places—can change the shape of the world. We publish poets and writers and renegades who stand outside of mainstream culture—poets, essayists, and storytellers whose work might withstand the scrutiny of crows and coyotes, those who are cryptic and floral, the crepuscular, and the queer-at-heart. We are more than just a publisher but a community of writers. Our mission is to produce books that can serve as a compass and map to all wayfarers through wild terrain.

WAYFARERBOOKS.ORG